Big Cats

Cheetah

Written by
Steve Goldsworthy

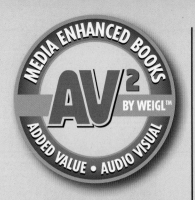

AV² provides enriched content that supplements and complements this book. Weigl's AV² books strive to create inspired learning and engage young minds in a total learning experience.

Your AV² Media Enhanced books come alive with...

Audio
Listen to sections of the book read aloud.

Key Words
Study vocabulary, and complete a matching word activity.

Video
Watch informative video clips.

Quizzes
Test your knowledge.

Go to www.av2books.com, and enter this book's unique code.

BOOK CODE

V439132

Embedded Weblinks
Gain additional information for research.

Slide Show
View images and captions, and prepare a presentation.

AV² by Weigl brings you media enhanced books that support active learning.

Try This!
Complete activities and hands-on experiments.

... and much, much more!

Published by AV² by Weigl
350 5th Avenue, 59th Floor
New York, NY 10118
Websites: www.av2books.com   www.weigl.com

Library of Congress Cataloging-in-Publication Data

Goldsworthy, Steve, author.
 Cheetah / Steve Goldsworthy.
     pages cm. -- (Big cats)
 Includes index.
 ISBN 978-1-4896-0910-6 (hardcover : alk. paper) -- ISBN 978-1-4896-0911-3 (softcover : alk. paper) --
ISBN 978-1-4896-0912-0 (single user ebk.) -- ISBN 978-1-4896-0913-7 (multi user ebk.)
 1. Cheetah--Juvenile literature. I. Title.
 QL737.C23G643 2015
 599.75'9--dc23
                                        2014004525

Printed in the United States of America in North Mankato, Minnesota
1 2 3 4 5 6 7 8 9 0 18 17 16 15 14

032014
WEP150314

Editor Heather Kissock and Megan Cuthbert   Design Terry Paulhus

Contents

Meet the Cheetah

Cheetahs are one of the smaller cats in the big cat family. They are the fastest **mammal** on Earth. In fact, when they run at their top speeds, they can be faster than most cars. Cheetahs use their speed for hunting. They are **predators** that hunt other animals for food. Cheetahs can find **prey** from far away because of their excellent eyesight.

At one time, cheetahs lived all over Africa, India, and the Middle East. Some lived in China and even North America. Now they can be found only in parts of Africa and Asia. Few cheetahs still live in nature.

The word "cheetah" comes from the Hindi language. It means "spotted one."

All About
Cheetahs

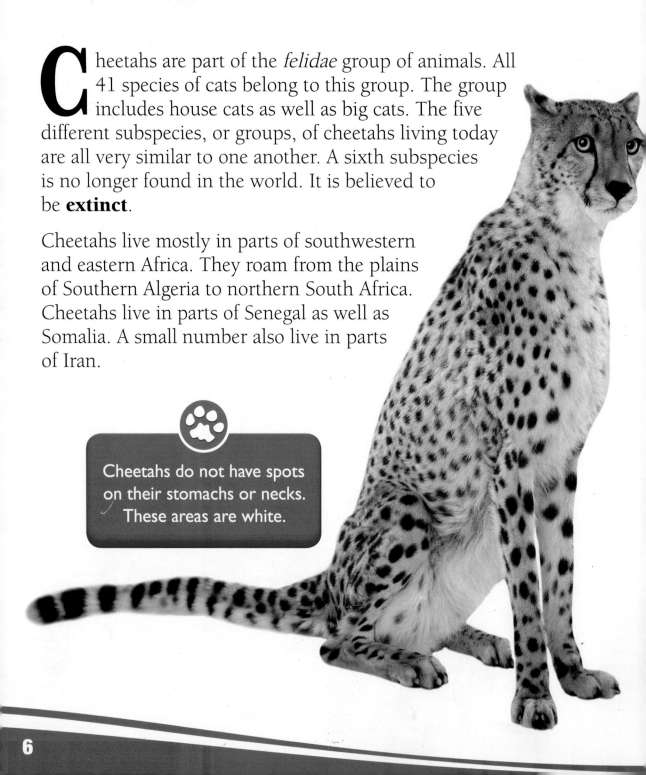

Cheetahs are part of the *felidae* group of animals. All 41 species of cats belong to this group. The group includes house cats as well as big cats. The five different subspecies, or groups, of cheetahs living today are all very similar to one another. A sixth subspecies is no longer found in the world. It is believed to be **extinct**.

Cheetahs live mostly in parts of southwestern and eastern Africa. They roam from the plains of Southern Algeria to northern South Africa. Cheetahs live in parts of Senegal as well as Somalia. A small number also live in parts of Iran.

Cheetahs do not have spots on their stomachs or necks. These areas are white.

Comparing Big Cats

The cheetah is different from other big cats. The larger cat species, such as the tiger, rely on size and strength to catch prey, while the cheetah relies on speed. It is built for quick and sudden turns to help catch its prey. The cheetah sprints toward its prey and knocks it to the ground.

Jaguar
+ **Length:**
7–9 feet
(213–274 centimeters)
including tail
+ **Weight:**
100–250 pounds
(45–113 kilograms)
+ **Speed:**
Up to 40 miles per hour
(64 kilometers
per hour)

Lion
+ **Length:**
6.5–9 feet
(198–274 cm)
including tail
+ **Weight:**
265–420 lbs
(120–190 kg)
+ **Speed:**
Up to 35 mph (56 kph)

Tiger
+ **Length:**
7.5–10.8 feet
(260–330 cm)
including tail
+ **Weight:**
220–675 pounds
(100–306 kg)
+ **Speed:**
Up to 40 mph (64 kph)

Leopard
+ **Length:**
6.5–9 feet
(198–274 cm)
including tail
+ **Weight:**
66–176 lbs (30–80 kg)
+ **Speed:**
Up to 57 mph (92 kph)

Cheetah
+ **Length:**
6–7 feet
(183– 213 cm)
including tail
+ **Weight:**
77–143 lbs (35– 65 kg)
+ **Speed:**
Up to 70 mph
(112 kph)

Cougar
+ **Length:**
5–9 feet
(152–274 cm)
including tail
+ **Weight:**
Up to 150 lbs (68 kg)
+ **Speed:**
Up to 35 mph (56 kph)

Cheetah History

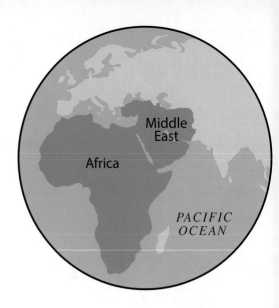

About 20,000 years ago, cheetahs were found in many areas of the world. Then, the world's climate changed at the end of the **Great Ice Age**. Many mammal species became extinct. The cheetah population became much smaller at this time. Cheetahs disappeared from many parts of the world. By the 21st century, cheetahs remained only in Africa and in parts of the Middle East.

Cheetahs were once kept as pets in Persia, which is now called Iran. Egyptian **pharaohs** also tamed cheetahs. In the fifth century, Europeans used cheetahs to hunt. In some countries, people even kept cheetahs as pets. One Indian ruler reportedly owned 9,000 cheetahs.

By the 19th century, the world's cheetah population dropped to 100,000. Many cheetahs could not find food or a place to live. Some cheetahs were killed by larger predators. Today, fewer than 10,000 cheetahs live in nature.

PREHISTORIC CHEETAH

Ancient **fossils** show that cheetahs lived in Texas, Nevada, and Wyoming more than 20,000 years ago.

8

The cheetah is now extinct in more than 20 countries.

Where Cheetahs Live

Most of the world's cheetah population is found in **sub-Saharan** Africa. This includes the countries of Tanzania, Botswana, Kenya, and Zimbabwe. Most cheetahs live in **protected** African parks, such as the Serengeti National Park. In these areas, cheetahs are safe from hunters. These parks are usually savannas, which are large, dry plains. They are covered in tall grasses, shrubs, and small trees. Cheetahs use these grasses and shrubs to hide while they stalk their prey.

The territory of a male cheetah can cover 14 square miles (36.26 square kilometers). The male will share its territory with two or three brothers. They will hunt in this territory together for life. A female cheetah travels alone, often through several male territories. Throughout the year, the female can roam across an area of up to 1,158.3 square miles (3,000 sq. km).

IN THE GRASS

Female cheetahs use tall grass to hide their young from predators. They will move their families every few days.

In Namibia, Africa, the government has set aside 28,000 acres (113.31 sq. km) of land to protect cheetahs.

Cheetah Features

Cheetahs are built for speed. They have slender bodies and long legs that make them natural sprinters. They also have small heads compared to the size of their bodies. This smaller head size makes them **streamlined** for running fast. Cheetah's spotted coat serves as **camouflage**. Their coats allow them to blend into the tall grass of the savanna.

Getting Closer

① Tail

- Can be up to 33 inches (84 cm)
- End covered in rings
- Helps them turn quickly
- Helps them maintain balance

② Coat

- Golden-yellow coat
- Has more than 2,000 black spots
- Has unique patterns
- "Tear stripes" on face

③ Throat

- Cannot roar
- Communicates with chirping noises
- Can be heard 1 mile (1.6 km) away
- Can also purr, moan, hiss, and growl

④ Hind Legs

- Can turn quickly
- Stride covers up to 25 feet (8 meters)
- Can complete three strides in one second

⑤ Paws

- Rough pads give traction
- Cannot fully **retract** claws
- Claws help grip the ground

③

⑤

What Do Cheetahs Eat?

Cheetahs are **carnivores**. They only eat meat that they have hunted. Their main prey are antelope and wild hare. They also eat impalas, wildebeest calves, and gazelles.

Cheetahs are daylight hunters. They do not hunt at night. Male cheetahs often hunt in packs. A female cheetah must hunt for her cubs. She also teaches her cubs to hunt for themselves.

When hunting, cheetahs leap from the grass and chase their prey. Then, they knock it down to make the kill. Cheetahs drag their kill to a shady area. Hunting is a difficult task, and cheetahs are often exhausted after a hunt.

Cheetahs sometimes prey on springbok, a type of antelope found throughout Africa.

FOOD FIGHT

Cheetahs must protect their kill from larger animals. Hiding food in tall grass helps keep other predators from spotting it.

Cheetah
Life Cycle

Cheetahs mate throughout the year. They may have different mates throughout their lifetime. A female cheetah can give birth to two to four cubs at a time. The cubs are born three months after mating.

Birth to 2 Weeks

Newborn cheetah cubs weigh between 9 and 15 ounces (255 and 425 grams). Their eyes open within 10 days. The cubs have gray fur with a ridge of long hair along their backs called a **mantle**. The mantle makes the cubs harder to see in tall grass.

Cheetah cubs spend their early years learning from their mother. They play with their littermates. This teaches them hunting techniques. A cheetah cub stays with its mother for up to two years. At two years old, females leave their family group. They are then old enough to mate and raise their own cubs.

2 Years and Older

At 2 years, a full-grown female cheetah is slightly smaller than a full-grown male cheetah. Female cheetahs usually live alone but will stay with their cubs for up to 2 years. Male cheetahs often live in small groups called **coalitions**. An adult cheetah can live 10 to 12 years.

2 Weeks to 2 Years

Cheetah cubs' teeth appear after 3 weeks. Cubs stop nursing from their mother and begin eating meat at 5 to 6 weeks. At about 7 weeks, the cubs are ready to hunt with their mother.

Conservation of Cheetahs

Only 7,000 to 10,000 cheetahs still live in nature. Cheetahs face many challenges in the different places they live. Hunters sometimes kill cheetahs for their spotted coats. Ranchers shoot cheetahs they believe have killed their livestock. Human settlers destroy the grasslands that cheetahs call home. Cheetahs are also losing their food sources. Hunters often kill other animals, such as antelope, that cheetahs hunt. This makes it hard for cheetahs to find food.

Cheetahs are an **endangered** species at risk of extinction. Organizations such as the DeWildt Cheetah and Wildlife Centre work to protect cheetahs. The Cheetah Conservation Fund educates local farmers so they can live peacefully with cheetahs. Efforts to preserve the cheetah's natural habitat will help the species survive.

KEEPING TRACK

The Serengeti Cheetah Project keeps track of individual cheetahs living on the plains of the Serengeti National Park.

People can drive through national parks across Africa to see cheetahs up close.

Myths and Legends

Wild animals play a part in local legends throughout the world. Many traditional African stories are about the cheetah. Native bushmen tell tales of why the cheetah runs so fast. Other myths try to explain why the cheetah has spots.

A **Zulu** story tells why the cheetah has black stripes down its face. A lazy hunter watched a female cheetah hunt. He was so impressed that he decided to steal the cheetah's three cubs and train them to hunt for him. When the mother discovered her babies were missing, she cried so hard that her tears left black marks on her face. To this day, stains on a cheetah's face remind hunters that they must hunt for themselves.

The cheetah is an important part of stories and myths in a number of cultures, including the Zulu culture.

What Makes a Cheetah Fast?

Scientists study cheetahs in the wild to learn what characteristics make them fast. They also study the characteristics of other fast animals. You can better understand what makes cheetahs fast by comparing them to other speedy animals.

Materials Needed: You will need a large piece of paper and markers.

STEP 1 List five fast land animals, including the cheetah, on the left side of the paper. These animals may include a horse or a greyhound dog. Research these animals using the internet and books. Draw a line across the paper under the name of each animal.

STEP 2 Use the information in this book to list characteristics that make the cheetah fast. These characteristics may include long legs or a small head. Write the characteristics across the bottom of the page. Draw lines down the page, creating columns.

Cheetah	✓	✓	✓	✓
Animal 1		✓		
Animal 2				
Animal 3				
Animal 4				
	Characteristic	Characteristic	Characteristic	Characteristic

STEP 3 Research each animal and put a check mark in the box above the characteristic it shares with cheetahs. Then, compare the characteristics of the cheetah to the characteristics of the other animals.

5 Know Your FACTS

Test your knowledge of cheetahs.

1 How far can a cheetah travel in one second?

2 How many cheetahs did one Indian ruler have as pets?

3 What makes cheetahs' paws unique?

4 How do cheetahs catch their prey?

5 What is the ridge of hair on a cheetah cub's back called?

Key Words

camouflage: markings that allow something to blend into its surroundings

carnivores: animals that eat only meat

coalitions: groups of persons or things working as one

endangered: in danger of no longer living on Earth

extinct: something that has died out or no longer exists

fossils: remains of a living thing, such as a footprint or bone, from a previous time period

Great Ice Age: a time when portions of Earth were covered in ice and glaciers

mammal: an animal that has fur and gives birth to live young

mantle: a pointy strip of hair along the back of the cheetah cub

pharaohs: kings of ancient Egypt

predators: animals that hunt other animals as food

prey: an animal hunted for food by another animal

protected: guarded from danger, attack, or harm

retract: to draw back or pull in

streamlined: shaped to reduce air resistance while moving

sub-Saharan: a region in Africa south of the Sahara desert

Zulu: a group of people living in South Africa who share the same language and culture

Index

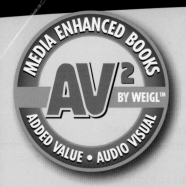

Log on to www.av2books.com

AV² by Weigl brings you media enhanced books that support active learning. Go to www.av2books.com, and enter the special code found on page 2 of this book. You will gain access to enriched and enhanced content that supplements and complements this book. Content includes video, audio, weblinks, quizzes, a slide show, and activities.

AV² Online Navigation

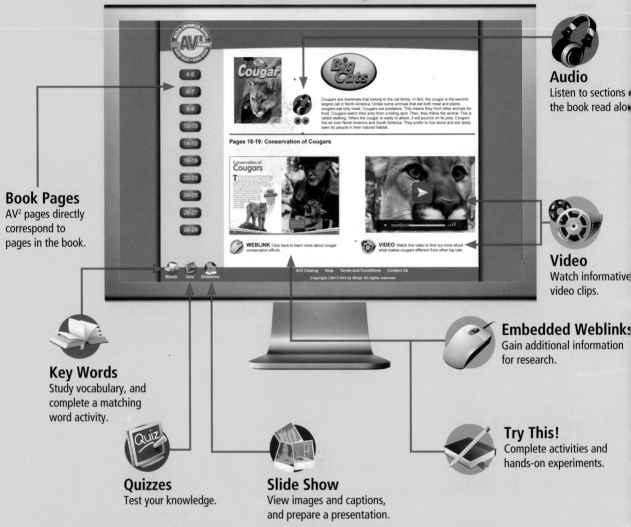

Book Pages
AV² pages directly correspond to pages in the book.

Audio
Listen to sections of the book read aloud.

Video
Watch informative video clips.

Key Words
Study vocabulary, and complete a matching word activity.

Embedded Weblinks
Gain additional information for research.

Quizzes
Test your knowledge.

Slide Show
View images and captions, and prepare a presentation.

Try This!
Complete activities and hands-on experiments.

AV² was built to bridge the gap between print and digital. We encourage you to tell us what you like and what you want to see in the future.

Sign up to be an AV² Ambassador at www.av2books.com/ambassador.